US ARMED FORCES

JOIN THE ARMY

By P. P. Mitchell

HOT TOPICS

Gareth Stevens
PUBLISHING

Please visit our website, www.garethstevens.com. For a free color catalog of all our high-quality books, call toll free 1-800-542-2595 or fax 1-877-542-2596.

Library of Congress Cataloging-in-Publication Data

Names: Mitchell, P. P., author.
Title: Join the Army / P. P. Mitchell.
Description: New York : Gareth Stevens Publishing, [2018] | Series: US armed
  forces | Includes index.
Identifiers: LCCN 2016057857| ISBN 9781538205341 (pbk. book) | ISBN
  9781538205358 (6 pack) | ISBN 9781538205365 (library bound book)
Subjects: LCSH: United States. Army--Juvenile literature. | United States.
  Army--Vocational guidance--Juvenile literature.
Classification: LCC UA25 .M655 2018 | DDC 355.0023/73--dc23
LC record available at https://lccn.loc.gov/2016057857

Published in 2018 by
Gareth Stevens Publishing
111 East 14th Street, Suite 349
New York, NY 10003

Copyright © 2018 Gareth Stevens Publishing

Designer: Bethany Perl
Editor: Joan Stoltman

Photo credits: Photos courtesy of US Army: cover, p. 1 Staff Sgt. Pablo N. Piedra, p. 5 by 1st Lt. Henry Chan, p. 7 by Sgt. Ryan Hallock, p. 9 by eagle1effi, p. 15 by Staff Sgt. Teddy Wade, p. 17 by Staff Sgt. Timothy Koster, pp. 19, 27 by Staff Sgt. Russell Lee Klika, p. 21 by Sgt. Luisito Brooks, p. 23 by www.army.mil/medalofhonor/petry, p. 29 by Sgt. Mark Scovell, p. 30 (combat uniform) by Staff Sgt. Brandon Moreno; cover, p. 1-32 (camouflage) Chikumaya/Wikipedia.org; cover, pp. 1-32 (grunge effect) iulias/Shutterstock.com; cover, pp. 1-32 (rounded text box) foxie/Shutterstock.com; cover, pp. 1-31 (border) jumpingsack/Shutterstock.com; pp. 2-32 (text box) Olga_C/Shutterstock.com; pp. 5-29 (dog tag) Feng Yu/Shutterstock.com; p. 11 PATRICK BAZ/AFP/Getty Images; p. 13 Chris Hondros/Getty Images News/Getty Images; p. 15, 21 (American Flag) Nataliia K/Shutterstock.com; pp. 25, 30 (mess dress uniform) The U.S. Army/Wikipedia.org; p. 30 SGM Phil Prater/Wikipedia.org.

Printed in China

CPSIA compliance information: Batch #CS17GS: For further information contact Gareth Stevens, New York, New York at 1-800-542-2595.

CONTENTS

ALL ABOUT THE ARMY

The army is the biggest armed force in the United States, made up of 700,000 people called soldiers. Soldiers are often the first armed forces sent into a war or battle for the United States.

DID YOU KNOW?

The first army in the United States was the Continental army, created in 1775. George Washington was the first leader of the army before he was president!

SOLDIERS ALL OVER THE WORLD!

Bases are places where an armed force is set up. Our country has 79 army bases. There are also bases in 74 other countries. As a soldier, you'll be relocated, or moved, to the base that needs your skills and talents.

DID YOU KNOW?

In the United States, bases are a lot like small towns. They have restaurants, gyms, grocery stores, movie theaters, libraries, churches, parks, and more!

WHAT WILL MY JOB BE?

The army has jobs in lots of different fields! Soldiers fly helicopters and drive tanks, but also perform **maintenance** on them. They may program computers, plan bridges, guard bases and weapons, build roads, and much more.

DID YOU KNOW?

You'll need to pass flight-school training to be able to fly army helicopters. After training and practicing flying for many hundreds of hours, you'll be able to fly on all types of **missions**!

Soldiers can also be nurses, builders, and more. They may work in an office, making sure there's enough food, water, and fuel on base. Or they might work ordering new parts and making sure repairs are done on time.

DID YOU KNOW?

Soldiers in the army get to work with a lot of really cool tools and maybe even help invent new things! **Drones**, for example, have been used by the army since World War I (1914–1918) and have become a big part of wars fought today.

HOW DO I JOIN?

There are two different ways to join the army: enlisting or training to become an officer. Enlisting, or joining by choice, means you'll be trained to do a certain job. Being an officer means planning missions and giving enlisted soldiers orders to get missions done.

DID YOU KNOW?

You can enlist at age 18 or at age 17 if your parent agrees. **Recruiters** like to meet parents so they know you've talked about this big choice with your family.

ENLISTING

When enlisting, you'll first speak to a recruiter. Then you'll take a test that measures skills and knowledge to see what jobs you'd be good at. After that, you'll have a physical, or a test of your body, eyes, and hearing.

ENLISTED ARMY RANKS

SERGEANT MAJOR OF THE ARMY
COMMAND SERGEANT MAJOR
SERGEANT MAJOR
FIRST SERGEANT
MASTER SERGEANT
SERGEANT FIRST CLASS
STAFF SERGEANT
SERGEANT
CORPORAL
SPECIALIST
PRIVATE
FIRST CLASS
PRIVATE

ARNTSON   U.S.ARMY

DID YOU KNOW?

Enlisted soldiers and officers have two different sets of ranks, or titles that show how much responsibility one has. Officers always rank higher than enlisted soldiers.

15

After you enlist, you'll go to basic combat training for 10 weeks. If you pass all parts of this training, you'll graduate and become an enlisted soldier! From there, you'll go straight to advanced individual training, where you'll learn your job.

DID YOU KNOW?

Enlisted soldiers can move up in rank and become an officer by going through even more training!

BECOMING AN OFFICER

You can become an officer during college in two ways. You can join the Reserve Officers' Training Corps (ROTC) at over 1,100 colleges. Or, you can go to the United States Military Academy—also called West Point—in New York.

DID YOU KNOW?
Presidents Ulysses S. Grant and Dwight D. Eisenhower were both West Point graduates and army leaders. Their leadership and success in the army helped them get elected president!

You can become an officer after graduating from 4-year college, too. You can go to officer training school at Fort Benning, Georgia. Or, you can go to special training after graduating from law or medical school.

DID YOU KNOW?

Being an officer isn't easy. Officers make important decisions during hard times and are responsible for the soldiers they lead.

ARMY OFFICER RANKS

GENERAL OF THE ARMY

GENERAL

LIEUTENANT GENERAL

MAJOR GENERAL

BRIGADIER GENERAL

COLONEL

LIEUTENANT COLONEL

MAJOR

CAPTAIN

FIRST LIEUTENANT

SECOND LIEUTENANT

SPECIAL OPERATIONS: THE RANGERS

Rangers are highly trained soldiers who work in small groups that specialize in sudden attacks and saving lives in battle with few tools. They have to be smart in many ways, including quickly learning the language of places they're sent!

DID YOU KNOW?
After basic ranger training, you'll keep training and learning. You'll learn how to jump out of planes, swim long distances, escape capture, and much more!

23

SPECIAL OPERATIONS: THE SPECIAL FORCES

Special Forces are some of the top soldiers in the army. They have over a year of training, including 24 weeks of learning other languages and **cultures**, and 15 weeks learning the Special Forces job they've been given.

DID YOU KNOW?

Special Forces, usually called the Green Berets, train people in other countries to fight, steal enemy weapons and information, save trapped soldiers, and spy.

WOMEN IN THE ARMY

Since the Revolutionary War, women have helped the army as nurses, cooks, and secretaries—with no pay and without even being asked to help! Over time, new laws passed that allowed women any job in the army.

DID YOU KNOW?

In 2016, the first women **armor** officers, rangers, and **infantry** officers graduated training.

HOW CAN I GET READY NOW?

Exercising every day and eating healthy are great ways to practice for the army. Study and do your homework to get good grades. As a friend, classmate, neighbor, brother or sister, son or daughter, be loyal, brave, respectful, and honest.

THE WARRIOR ETHOS

I Will Always Place the Mission First.

I Will Never Accept Defeat.

I Will Never Quit.

I Will Never Leave a Fallen Comrade.

DID YOU KNOW?

You can also prepare for the army by learning and practicing "The Warrior Ethos," a short piece of writing that tells what soldiers try to do in the army.

ARMY UNIFORMS

COMBAT UNIFORM

SERVICE UNIFORM

DRESS MESS UNIFORM

FOR MORE INFORMATION

Books

Alvarez, Carlos. *Army Rangers*. Minneapolis, MN: Bellwether Media, 2010.

Goldish, Meish. *Army: Civilian to Soldier*. New York, NY: Bearport Publishing, 2011.

Gordon, Nick. *U.S. Army*. Minneapolis, MN: Bellwether Media, 2013.

Websites

Army Know-How: Exploring the Army Field Manual
thenmusa.org/army-know-how.php#
Read all about how to be in the army.

U.S. Army
goarmy.com
Explore the army's official website.

GLOSSARY

armor: tanks and the soldiers who watch the enemy and plan attacks

culture: the beliefs and ways of life of a group of people

drone: an unmanned aircraft that is controlled by someone on the ground

infantry: enlisted soldiers trained to use arms and fight in land battles

maintenance: the labor of fixing something or keeping it in good working shape

mission: a task or job a group must perform

recruiter: a person in a community who helps people join the armed forces

INDEX